THE LURE OF
IMPERMANENCE

Poems

Carey Taylor

Carey Taylor

ISBN: 978-1722669041
First Printing July 2018
Printed in the U.S.A.

Editing: Michael Burwell
            Sandra Kleven
Cover: Photo from the author's collection
Design: Vered R. Mares, VP&D House

Published by

CIRQUE PRESS

Sandra Kleven – Michael Burwell
3978 Defiance Street
Anchorage, AK 99504
Anchorage, Alaska

cirquejournal@gmail.com
cirquejournal.com

For Charles, who knows the distance we must travel.

ACKNOWLEDGMENTS

Special thanks to the editors of the following publications where these poems first appeared, sometimes in different versions.

Cirque-A Literary Journal for the North Pacific Rim: "The Algol Paradox," "Arrivals and Departures," "Heirlooms," "Pomology Lessons," "The White Album Summer," "Mental Illness in America," "Pangaea Lost," "Sicks Stadium, July 5th, 1970," "As I Watch the Wake from the Deck of the Edmonds Ferry," and "After"

Clover - A Literary Rag: "Finally Becoming Gaia," "Removal of the English Elms," "Wash Day with Grandma," "Math That Doesn't Add Up," and "Fault Lines"

Off the Coast: "Not Another Morning"

Shark Reef-A Literary Magazine: "Elegy"

Brevity Poetry Review: "Pieces of Light"

Snapdragon: A Journal of Art and Healing: "At the Musée d'Orsay"

Poetry Corners 2014: Do Not Be Afraid: "Where Pain Takes Flight"

Dodging the Rain (Ireland): "Sylvia Plath Watches a Young Woman in Checkout Line at Walmart," "Post-Election," "Treeline," "Blessing," and "Boat Basin Blues"

New York Times Blog - Donald Trump Poetry Contest: "American as Apple Pie"

DEDICATION

Heartfelt thanks to all the poets who were kind and encouraging to me from the beginning, but special thanks to John Willson of Bainbridge Island whose poetry workshops were invaluable to me, to Gary Lilley and Michael D'Alessandro of the Writers' Workshop in Port Townsend whose poetry workshops expanded my craft, to Nancy Rekow and the entire *Ars Poetica* crew who gave me opportunities to read my work, to the late Joan Swift whose courage to speak her truth was a model to me, and most of all to the amazing Sandra Kleven and Michael Burwell of Cirque Press, who know how important it is to create a community of artists who support each other—for that and so much more, I say thank you, thank you, thank you.

Thanks to all my friends and family who share their stories and encourage mine. This journey would not have been as lovely had you not been part of it.

Thanks to Lesley and Sean for being the best cheerleaders any Mom could wish for. Thanks for letting me read my poems with the band and for driving great distances to hear me read.

Thanks to my dad for showing me the Ireland of Yeats and Heaney and to my mom for reading me the poem "The Babes in the Wood" which broke my five-year-old heart wide open.

Special thanks to Georgia Rae Lennon my high school English teacher, who published my first poems in a school chapbook and encouraged me to keep writing.

With love and gratitude to my husband Charles, who understands the need to tell one's story and isn't afraid to reinvent a life together. Your unfailing support has made this chapter of my life all the richer.

Contents

III. American as Apple Pie

IV. Places We Travel

I.

Arrivals and Departures

Sylvia Plath Watches a Young Woman in Checkout Line at Walmart

are you blue?

not like
egg of robin

blue-black blue
before heal of bruise

midnight
cave of bat

inky
of deepest ocean

      carbon blue of knife
      you slide between

leaving
      and
          gone

oh let me fill your cart with
what mine cannot hold—

cobalt of nebula

turquoise of Navajo

cornflower of child's barrette

      cerulean blue of sky
      you reach for after

coming
      and
          here

Elegy

She is the absence of light
at the edge of the door
        bruise of sky on the horizon
caw of crow
letter never written.

Once a white communion dress
anthology of poems
        beaded bracelets gold and green
dough of pie
cinnamon sugar sprinkle.

Arrivals and Departures

Even with her daughter dead
the cottonwoods in the ravine
left a downy shroud on the windows
while we sat in chairs
and fingered fabrics
for families
yet unscathed.

Even with her daughter dead
she appeared on my door
with a double tall latte
while the ferry in the harbor moaned
arrivals and departures
as if silent cancer cells multiplying
weren't enough.

Even with her daughter dead
the tormented squall sailed toward shore
while birds sang without remorse
and thick spring rain
torrent tearing up the street
brought hope on a stem
in the name of trillium and iris.

As I Watch the Wake from the Deck
of the Edmonds Ferry

——*For Joan Swift*

you've become the *silt*
              you run over   *the willow root*
                    you unwind

pink of Plumeria washed up
              on a black sand beach
                    purple jacket   the color of lilacs

top beginning to wobble,
              manuscript on a kitchen table,
                    narrative shaped in stanza and

line   where you dazzle your way through
              a tunnel of sorrow
                    body of all this water

where you still rise *to the surface*
              and take *the breath*
                    we who are left

are *still breathing* for you

What the Artist Does

Year 1

Two weeks before Christmas
her mother died.

After the movers were gone, she wailed alone—
then panicked, the boxes weren't taped tight enough.

Year 2

She stood barefoot on her mother's rug
and painted a small white canvas.

By December, even the walls
of her studio.

Pomology Lessons

1

Out the 9th floor window
the sky is filled with
oyster light.
Clouds migrate,
buildings exhale,
morphine drips.

2

My father pulls the nurse aside
asks how long before his wife can go home,
explains they have pies to bake.
Before she can answer
he begins a lecture on Liberty Apple pomology.
He describes deep red skin with fleshly yellow insides.
Praises their hardiness and vigor.
Elucidates her on their one demand of well-drained soil.
When he senses the nurse become bored, he becomes
animated – especially at the part about low disease susceptibility,
how they are foolproof really,
reliable, well balanced,
and sweet.

3

Back home in their garage
are bags of yesterday's apples, tree limbs unfettered,
fruit resting ripe, on cold cement.

Heirlooms

The Fourth of July roses
hang from my father's arbor
        sweet apple first   then ruffles
red and white   with buttery bean sprout centers.

Worn linen petals   flutter   flutter
and wave welcome   inviting one last
look   before canes are frozen
streams   or seed pods   bird-picked clean.

As I leave   we tarry   tarry
at the trellis. He admires how far
they've grown   touches them tenderly
turns and asks   again

aren't they something?

As if I didn't hear him on all my previous visits
as if   I don't understand what he is saying to me
as if   in the gloaming summer fade
I somehow miss   the flicker

in his eyes,
after he snips
        then hands over
that pinwheel jewel.

As if   in his eighty-year-old
hand   I cannot see
his mother's
crooked finger.

Pieces of Light

The brain MRI scan is the most useful test for confirming the diagnosis of Multiple Sclerosis. MS lesions appear as areas of high signal, predominantly in the cerebral white matter or spinal cord.
—American Academy of Family Physicians, 2004 Nov. 15

It starts so simply,
a toss of dead flowers
from a milk white vase
into the compost.

The reeking rot of life
an olfactory assault
I run from and to
a washing clean
over the sink,

where morning light
and translucent glass
become tender thought
of green days
and promises broken.

It started so simply,
a leg that didn't work
then two, so she came on four
with lovelies from her garden.

Removal of the English Elms

—Bloedel Reserve, November 2013

Everything takes its leaving. Tomorrow
with blades sharp   it will be the English Elms
in a careful   planned execution.

Before that it was the poet
not careful or planned   at all

this past summer
it was the eagle   with its aerie and tree
the holy trinity gone   when you arrived.

Yes, everything takes its leaving
even the Romans   with their suckers of
Ulmus procera   domesticating Britain.

So while you are here
lay your hand on a trunk   and maybe an ear

and listen.

Not Another Morning

A white cup.
A silver kettle.
A black crow.

A thick heart.
Crusts of bread.
A blue toe.

A mossy bed.
Track of bear.
The sun low.

Swimming Laps (and Because You Loved Sonnets)

In darkest dreams I find you every night,
You walk through our door then sit next to me.
Your eyes soft and clear spark of our last fight,
Those golden days before, coins lost at sea.
Last rites are never done, hurts seldom gone,
And my abject words cannot bridge the gap.
Music we once wrote fades away from song,
So I flip a turn, start another lap,
Stroke through the blue where anguish can let go,
Hold you like before drops of death began,
Watch with clearer eyes all your goodness show,
From our secret spot by the windy strand.
Then scan swirl of tide in that vast marine,
Beg briny air to blow us back to green.

II.

Between Roof and Sky

Boat Basin Blues

On the boat,
it's only crest, trough,
roll of cloud,
            distant horizon.

At the marina,
dock lines
tied,
he finds them
waiting on their bellies—
arms dangling
in the oily green,
fingers poking
sea anemones, that
cling to pilings like they
now attach to his legs—
and where in the stench
of diesel and diaper,
he feels the heavy drag
            of their tuna weight.

Childhood Lessons in Charleston, Oregon

Praise the skunk cabbage green and gold,
the damp and putrid air,
praise the push and heat of spathe,
and the bite I gave you.

Praise brown eyes that said *betrayed,*
and your mouth that spat,
praise the bitter on my tongue,
sting of small lips burning.

Praise my hand that touched your back,
the mud between our toes,
praise the slip and slime of bank,
the creek-song filled with toad.

Praise the skunk cabbage green and gold,
the damp and putrid air,
praise the push and heat of spathe
the crack of one heart breaking.

Fault Lines

I am born at the sandy edge
of the Southern Oregon coast.

Winter storms heave forests of Bull Kelp
onto the beach.

Grays migrate south from the icy Bering Sea
to warm lagoons in Baja.

As I lie in my crib, offshore in the Pacific,
Cascadia is *locked and loaded.*

*

I am nine when the news of an earthquake in Alaska
will tap itself known on the teletype.

My father will shake us from sleep with orders
to evacuate the Coast Guard Station.

My brother will fetch our dog.
My mother will drive the curved darkness

up Seven Devils Road,
pull over, then silently wait.

*

When I am eighteen, my mother and I watch the taillights
of my father's car, slip down our gravel driveway.

When the aftershocks come, I begin collecting
items for a survival kit.

With each addition—matches, water, knife, compass—
I pretend I am prepared for the full rip

and that what is unseen beneath the surface
won't split my world wide open.

The Divorce

It was a fragile binding
that kept them together.

Not duct-tape strong
but onionskin thin.

Torn with the first strong wind.
Flattened by the gales of not forgiving.

The depths of hate a tsunami force
the children were powerless against.

A familial unraveling. A thin thread as
distant and unreachable, as the bloodied

cord that had bound them together.

After

Because only 59% of the Moon's surface
is visible from Earth

I am reminded how little
you know of me.

The broom in my hand
is not about clean

sofa pillows plumped
not about neat

carpet vacuumed
a path to somewhere else.

And if you ask
(and you never have)

why a clean house
is so important to me

I will tell
you this—

with scrub of tile
black dissolves

in polish of chrome
reflection returns

on clean sheets
sanctuary found

that as our world spins
off its axis

a tidy house
is the only thing

I manage to keep
well-tended.

Reading Labels in the Pantry

They say too little folic acid during pregnancy
can be a cause of heart defects.

Which might explain my copious need for
D-3, my low blood pressure, my skipped beats.

The Simple Truth instant oatmeal in the pantry
claims to be transparent. I don't believe it.

The packaged quinoa is more honest.
Serve warm or chilled.

*

I am a boisterous Italian who craves the
Sicilian sun like the heat of an argument.

My mouth is a red chili pepper,
hot and spicy, subtly sweet, which causes

my mother to wring her pasta-floured hands on her
dirty apron and wail as I walk away—

my bambino,
my bambino,

always forgetting to give me tips on
how to cool angel food cake.

Redemption

I.

Be prepared
to lose the prickly pear beer you discovered in Sedona
at the Mexican restaurant with dried salsa on the table
which you scraped off with your nail
as the baby crab-pinched crumbs
off the chip-infested carpet
and the face
across the table
no longer
your Black Madonna.

II.

How many booths did you sit in?
How many beers between you?
How did you leave that sticky seat and end up on the shore
hair filled with
algae, clam, crab bits broken?
And when the tide still didn't turn
how did you walk off the jetty into the swirl
swim to that well-worn edge
and on your belly
let the small waves rock you?

Wash Day with Grandma

Absent something to read at the table
I chew slow, listen hard, as Simon and Garfunkel
sing: *doing laundry, hanging out shirts in the dirty breeze*

     which snaps
               my memory to release

as words move on and I stay back—mesmerized
by the wringer-washer on the cabin deck with
its frothy tub of bleach and dirt.

She scouts small fingers near the hem of her dress,
feeds work shirts between rollers which fall stiff in a tub,
holds clothespins with her teeth, while a Steller's jay

yaks in the skinny fir and rhododendrons
pop pink on the trail to the lake—
all of us ready to burst, in that rare bit of sun.

Of the Kestner Type

In the glitter of the year
I live next door to my grandmother

she will stand beside the tub
and tend my blistered feet

burnt black in the buried heat
of an old bonfire.

She will glare at my grandfather
his refusal to take me to town,

and when he returns with my brother
and two empty A & W mugs, she,

whom I have never seen drive,
will march to the back of their tiny trailer,

grab her stiff brocade purse and blue windbreaker,
step outside and quietly tell me to *get in the car.*

We will drive 10 slow miles down Highway 101,
where she will pull in next to drive-in speakers,

press the service button, and order two,
large, root beer floats.

On July 4th, she will fry her famous donuts our
collective kin hanker for, hand me the first greasy

brown bag, then shoo me outside
where I eat them alone in the agate beds.

She will wrap the 7-inch All-Bisque doll I covet as a child
in white tissue, then place her in a pink Avon box

that smells of rose talc, with a note written in blue ink
on white-lined paper describing its many features:

peach tone cheeks, angel wing lips, orange one-strap slippers,
brown sleep eyes made of glass.

Which when I am grown, she will place
in my hands as she lay dying,

still perfect in its silence.

Blessing

Her mother's voice comes out of the ether
like a chariot headed for Rome.

I have something to tell you.
Something splendid.

I know you think I'm prim,
that I always talk of sin,

but there was a time,
I lived for shenanigans,

draped my breasts in silk,
was wild to be shallow.

So   you too
                should go

past the orchard
        with its lemons and chickens

                to where air is tang of oregano
and light

        scatter
                of prism

Where Pain Takes Flight

What she remembers
is her head on her mother's lap
and the pine out the window

and though she had climbed its limbs all summer
only then did she see how it stood solitary
how it had begun to lean from the constant west wind.

What she remembers
is liquid cold and shocking poured in her aching ear
where it boiled up and out in a warm crackling
wiped dry with an old towel
as it trickled down her neck.

What she remembers
is the gentle stroke of her forehead
and her hair being pushed
from her eyes.

Between Roof and Sky

The teapot whistles on the burner,
my mother pours boiling water in two white cups,
        asks if I want sugar.

We crowd silence
with idle chitchat,
        talk on the rim of our grief.

Does she like her new car? What has my aunt been up to?
How about this string of hot days unending?
        Are her lung scans still clear?

I take a last sip, walk to the sink,
place my empty cup
        in the pile of dirty dishes.

And like the swallow outside the window
that tries over and over to find the gap in the eaves
        that got boarded up last summer,

I too, keep looking for a way back—
to that short-lived space
        between roof and sky.

III.

AMERICAN AS APPLE PIE

The White Album Summer

it was the summer she wanted holy communion
with the neighbor boy more than the body of
Christ wanted the hands of a lover to map her
body wrist to wrist then nail it to a future where
she could never forget she was the heat wave
through October a *wild honey pie* of pores that
oozed over-ripe peach a *cool cherry cream* looking
for *happiness* in a *warm gun* a girl who *broke the
rules deep in the jungle* of an old van hips moving to
a repeating soundtrack a repeating soundtrack
muffled between twin bed sheets where she
unfolded her girlhood with ears cocked to the
slam of a mother's car door and though she
never did *it in the road* there was the forest
behind her house where she came *out to play* then
walked home to bathe in brackish green water

Metamorphosis

On the grey cement stoop
sitting shiva on her lap
is a yellow frayed journal.

The Skagit Valley sky is salmon-egg orange.
The air on her skin frying pan hot.
Pores ooze eagerness waiting for a boy.

He drives a white Ford Falcon,
with a pomegranate red bench seat,
which they fill like a too-tight bra.

As he rounds the corner, she runs to the car,
slides her Levi covered legs in beside him.
Tucks his green eyes, between blue lined paper.

As they pull away from the curb
she rolls down the window,
gulps the ambrosia of peachy air

plunges her fluttering arm
into that August
inferno

pitches her childhood
to the black
exhaust.

Sicks Stadium, July 5th, 1970

The young ones arrive early
walk to the white monolith
        push through turnstiles
                in fringed vests and beads
enter the green field
with serape blankets
        and weed.

Joplin arrives by helicopter
her bottle of Southern Comfort
        already half empty
                on stage she belts out
Me and Bobby McGee
mouth wide open
        bracelets jingling.

Thirty minutes in—pissed the sound system
isn't right—she storms off the stage
        in her final exit from Seattle
                while you are deep in a smoky kiss
with a boy you just met
and bruised lips smudge a future
        where none of you exist.

Fidalgo Island at Fifteen

trespassing the golf course in early morning hours sprinklers sur-
prised them with a warm-cold soaking hand in hand they ran
and hopscotched puddles returning to the safety of their secret
sanctuary—while her father watched the clock and chain smoked
on the porch their weather-making universe was dripping down the
windows

Post-Election

At first they fed in multitudes, from
the high energy suet cube, hung
in the contorted filbert.

Then came week
upon week
of 20-degree weather.

At the icy shoulder of road,
a chickadee in daytime
torpor.

By the third week,
five feathered corpses
on frosted asphalt.

Who knew so many would not survive
that winter, next to the bay with its
foraging wetlands

or now, how much we need them,
to rise like Lazarus and sing
their sapphire songs.

Mental Illness in America

—Reynolds High School Shooting, May 2014

After my eyes welled wet,
after my Facebook post about
violence, teachers, fear,

after watching a reporter
interview a kid in shock
wondering where his sister was,

after hearing the gym teacher
was fine,
the bullet *only* grazed his hip,

I caught myself looking at my toes
noticed I needed a pedicure, thought
Popsicle Pink, would match my new blouse.

Math That Doesn't Add Up

—Umpqua Community College Shooting,
Roseburg, Oregon, September 2015

This morning my son rode his bicycle
to class at an Oregon college campus

sat at a desk calculating algorithms
while 110 miles south near Roseburg

a mother got the news her child had been
shot to death in Introductory Writing.

If an algorithm is a formal set of steps to solve
a problem, could someone please calculate

the number of safe days my boy can attend school
before the rules of sentence structure degrade to

writing poems in blood? And if the syllabus now reads:
taking this class may be hazardous to your health

is there a formula I can use to decide when to
withdraw him from class?

And while you are busy crunching numbers
how about solving this one—are the mentally ill

just the hunters or the hunted? A collective club
we join each time we hear a child weep, look them

in the eye and spin another tale of hope. Because tomorrow,
we know, in another town there will be another shooting

and all our promises of safekeeping
are lies.

9 to 5

—For every #MeToo

Work is a jungle you machete
your way through.

The snake on the vine
hides in the dark canopy
ready to slither its way
around your neck, but in
the downpour, you neither
see nor hear it.

Then screech of monkey.

Scream of jaguar.

Finally, the slash, slash, slash
of your roughshod blazing path.

Marshmallow Roast with Celtic Goddess Áine

heat of fire
smells like thunder

billow of smoke
grinds like coffee

dance of flame
cracks like ice

tang of tongue
thick like mallow

rub of sand
burns like acid

bite of ear
roars like ocean

American as Apple Pie

A word to the wise
Big brother is watching
Chomping at the bit

Dressed to kill
Eyes in the back of his head
Full of fake news

Get your ducks in a row
Have the last laugh
In the nick of time

Jump in with both feet
Keep your chin up
Let the good times roll

More than one way to skin a cat
Nip it in the bud
Open a can of worms

Push the envelope
Quicker than a New York minute
Rome wasn't built in a day

Seize the moment
Take one for the team
Upset the apple cart

Variety is not always the spice of life
When all is said and done
Xenophobe man

You don't miss the water till the well runs dry
Zig don't zag
Zig don't zag

IV.

Places We Travel

Places We Travel

At Austin Airport we wait for our flight to Seattle—sit
connected on black vinyl chairs prop feet on dirty luggage
flinch at static yammer of flight delays and boardings

talk on cell phones stare straight ahead play crossword puzzles
eat submarine sandwiches read books and magazines
hold the hand of an old woman as paramedics take her

blood pressure insert tubes of oxygen into her nose
place strong fingers feather light on wrists paper thin
speak in low and soothing voices.

When she apologizes for being ill the youngest of them
places his hand on her shoulder, looks into her eyes and
drawls, *No need to apologize Mam.*

As he ministers on bended knee, I want to
run my hand through his blonde crew cut hair—
remember my son's four-year-old head

with its play-hard heat just below the bristle—
want to empty my bag and repack my life
for one more kid-filled summer

where holiness was washing
grubby feet and a bike
in the yard.

Family Reunion

On summer visits with his grandpa
they pick blueberries,
broil on sand skirting Lake Michigan,
stroll the farmer's market,
walk the dog,
eat Moose Tracks ice cream
after dinner.

When the boy grows up
they browse art galleries
and bookstores,
talk guitars and
girlfriends,
grill salmon on the
barbecue.

Before the boy leaves
they drive North
on Highway 31,
stop for lunch
at the country club,
visit the family plot
at Spring Lake Cemetery.

They stand side-by-side
at the granite headstone,
read the words *Baby Taylor,*
the boy takes a picture with
his phone,
not sure of his return
nor wanting to forget

the trees turning
from lime to canary,
or this tiny sugar
bone melt,
still seeping
in the last heat
of summer.

Upon Receiving a Picture of My Daughter in a Text Message

Like all the mothers before us
Irish, Welsh, French and Polish
a cauldron of shared and not-shared history—
we too, Dear Daughter, are changing the guard.

Following the ageless and aging march
we take our place in the lineup,
where your golden gleaming hair
blows straight to the enemy.

The call to arms? Mere pixels sent
as your birthright walnut crown
flows now a honey oak, and
in that instant our eyes meet

a one-way looking mind you—
the gilded age where you
unknowingly reside
commands the helm.

Demarcation line firmly drawn
in shining silver glass.
A gravity-pulled reflection.
A saline stink ebb tide.

A waning winter moon.

From the Archive of Regrets

She sits on a nest of dirty clothes in the laundry room for days.
Her guinea pig, quiet on her lap, refuses to eat or drink.

She strokes his smooth coat, reads him every Berenstain Bear book
she owns. Stories filled with problems this bear family always solves.

I wash and dry, wash and dry,
until my glasses fog.

On day three, her father wraps him in an old tee shirt,
buries him in the backyard near the columbine and sweet peas.

When she returns home from school, face bright as noon summer
sky, I watch her melt like butter in my heaviest pan.

I try to sugarcoat her loss, suggest a cross, a few prayers,
a ring around the rosary—I should know—you can't shroud grief.

I should have remembered the day my horse
tied to a tree, tangled in her lead and broke her leg—

how the rural vet said *the right thing to do is put her down.*
I should have remembered the velvet of her muzzle,

foam *lathered beach runs*, tannin eyes,
foal in her womb.

But only now do I throw off that thin veil—
stay put on that patch of grass,

place my arms like a vise around her thick neck,
bury my girl-face in her mud-clotted mane.

The Algol Paradox

I.
Newton's First Law: Every object persists in its state of rest or uniform motion in a straightforward line

Imagine three-inch heels clack, clack, clacking
on the freshly waxed and polished floor,
see her crown just mown in a sexy boyish way.
Run your palms over her red race car hugging
curve of a dress, and inhale her perfume contrail,
a thick, sweet smothering on honey scent,
reeking of arrogance.

Now picture his back at the chalkboard. See his gray
wallet-worn corduroy pants and frayed clown suspenders,
walk about his head decaying and browse his bushy beard.
Watch him turn to face the class then speak his name.

Hover above us for an hour, as we watch with cataract-covered
eyes as the chalky green fills with equations. Sneak up behind us
and sniff fear in our silence. Read our thoughts: *The syllabus was
clear—no math prerequisites.* Understand we crave narrative not
numbers, of a universe unfolding—hoping that knowing a waxing
from waning moon might get us more than just a goodnight kiss as
we stumble home drunk in the early morning light.

unless it is compelled to change that state by forces impressed on it.

At first break notice the downcast eyes of her classmates as she
slowly stands up. See the short dress and high heels egging
her on as her syllabus shaking hand extracts an explanation.
Watch him squirm, confused, thinking the math isn't even difficult.
Understand her threat when she insists a course change is in order
if he wants them to return. Cringe as the child's wooden chair/
desk he is wedged in, strips him of any power he thought he might
possess. Watch her soften, as she looks into his eyes, saggy and
kind, as he tells her she has nothing to fear. Notice him stare at

her brick red lips, when she says *fine* in the snarly tone of the unenlightened.

Newton's Third Law: For every action (force) in nature there is an equal and opposite re-action.

In the dampness of your car, that eternal rainy spring, you will watch her return week after week, her posse in tow. You will doze in the back of the room, half listening to lectures on stellar evolution, the solar system, stars, the history of astronomy, comets, galaxies, and her favorite celestial neighbor—the Moon. On one cool, clear-sky evening, he will haul his telescope from the back of his moldy blue Ford Pinto (parked next to her new Audi) and you will see her face yield to an unseen force. Secretly you watch her eyes memorize his lanky, lean frame, his faded jeans with a knee emerging, his North Face jacket—cerulean blue that matches his eyes.

For her first view of the night sky, you will huff beside her on the way to the roof, eavesdropping as she whispers to her classmate girlfriend *well he seems to be a bit uptight, a bit uncomfortable in his own skin, but he does have a nice ass.* Her friend will cock her head, stare into her eyes and smugly laugh, *what he needs is a good fuck.* Her cheeks flood crimson as you hear her silent plan to beat her to the punch.

II.

Sirius,
Albireo,
Alpha Centauri,
Epsilon Lyrae,
their mysteries became my salvation,
their light-my hope,
their beauty-my desire,
their distance-my loneliness,
their teacher-my friend,
my lover,
my binary star,

the scientist who ripped
my world open,
the first time I looked
through the telescope lens
and he said
can you see them?
as I searched for the
Rings of Saturn
in the universe
that birthed me.
Thanking the Gods
I didn't believe in,
(yet how could I not)
for Einstein, Galileo, Newton,
the patient midwives,
who delivered me—
in one greedy gulping cosmic breath,
covered in stardust and blood,
to my beginning ending place—
that sweet black hole burial—

a mere star shooting by.

Thoughts While Waiting for My Husband to Return Home After Another Business Trip

When I read the poem *A Dog on His Master* by Billy Collins,
my thoughts didn't spark toward their short inch of time together,
but to questions like, who cleaned the shit off the grass

after a soft rain? Whose sleep was disturbed by a demanding
scratch at the door, and who bought the dog food and hauled
it to the car?

Questions that in turn ignited a brushfire in my brain
about poet laureate logistics. Like, who walked the dog
when he was gone? How was the chore puzzle divvied up

between bills on the counter and taxes to be filed? How
did *his favorite* red wine get freshly stocked in the pantry?
Or how does one return after days with poet groupies

standing in line for his signature, or from readings where
strangers bob their heads in dark auditoriums,
thinking they know *him?*

Not to mention those endless receptions thrown by others
for the chance to snuggle up to his brilliance.
But the question smoldering underneath it all, was

when he returned home to his familiar bathroom,
lifted the toilet seat and saw dry yellow dribble,
did he lower it quietly and walk out, or leave it up

in annoyed defiance? Or was there a sorrow in those
commonest of lost days, that brought him to his knees
to scour?

Her Husband Flies on the Stratospheric Observatory for Infrared Astronomy

Imagine a young boy with eyes clear blue
dressed for Halloween as Peter Pan,
Spock, or Daniel Boone.

A boy who reads Edgar Rice Burroughs
then pounds his chest like Tarzan in the
backyard horse chestnut.

A boy who annoys his classmates with
straight A's and his need
to be right.

A boy who dreams of becoming
an astronaut—heavens held earthbound
with wheezy lungs.

A boy who breaks his college swimming
records, bikes from Oregon to Michigan,
climbs scree and glacier to summit Mt. Hood.

A boy who gets his Ph.D. in physics because he could,
who gives his students lectures on astronomy, and meets his
future wife, between a waxing and waning moon.

A man who tethers himself to a daughter and son,
and brings their eyes to a telescope to view Cassiopeia,
Betelgeuse, and the orbit of a space shuttle.

A man who helps his son build a plywood spaceship,
which he will perch high on a shed roof in the back yard,
where they planet hop on summer nights.

Now imagine a man nearing sixty, who sits at a cubicle
in Silicon Valley and writes simulation software for a 100-inch
reflecting telescope mounted in a 747.

A man who after three years will finally sit in the cockpit
as it rolls down the desert runway, as close to his
dream of space as he will ever be in his lifetime.

A man who will view Arcturus
and the asteroid Aline from the world's
largest airborne observatory.

A man who after landing will disembark, turn and look back at
the plane sitting on the tarmac and watch the curve of sunrise
break in the east between its wings.

A man who knows the ocean of stardust our bodies contain
and the distance we must travel,
to be of earth.

Soviet Space Dog Lament

Oh Pup-nik
Oh Pooch-nik
Oh Sput-pup

Oh Woof-nik
Oh Mutt-nik
Oh Laika

Sirius welcomes you
        from small hot rockets
into the fish scale twinkle.

Oh Dog Star
Oh Moon Dog
Oh Wolf Star

Gather these most muted of lights
        peat moss a warm bed
cover them with your flickering

quilt,   until the night we lie
on our collective backs
        in all the yards   in all the world

and howl
to the infinite memory
        of the cosmos

Looking Both Ways

Silicon Valley boys on my right
sit in wheels bimmer bright.

The light is red.
Heads are down.

Palms hold phones.
Fingers fly.

A young woman on my left
slow climbs social service stairs.

Beads of sweat above her brow.
Tight grip on toddler's hand.

It's just another lunch hour
in this trafficky town.

Where food stamps and table lines
snake around blocks,

and a child's tattered
shoes, keep shuffling.

Hiking Together for Twenty Years

like the water from Falls Creek Falls
we have tumbled

at the beginning without fear
like all young things

now standing here
with the roar of water

and comfortable
friendship

in no hurry to turn
down the trail

or arrive at pools
dark and still

Treeline

He worries he won't get a job
after four years of coding
in dark rooms for a degree so fresh
it hasn't even been framed
properly. You want to tell him,
as if he were still a child,
and you his childhood mother,
this is not the worst thing,
this lack of a job,
because your inclination
is to problem solve, compile strengths,
list options. But before you can speak,
he changes the topic,
shares he hiked the Cascades
on a day so clear
he saw Hood, Adams, St. Helens,
and then there you are—
in the summer after your second
marriage ended, bagging mountain after
mountain, and how you did not know
in the lush of conifer and fern,
but at the windswept edge of
scree and scraggly pine, where
a Red-tailed hawk looped up and up.

Pangaea Lost

I drink my morning coffee
in empty homes and short sales.
Research annual rainfall,
bakeries, and bookstores.
At night I shore walk
and wake in other writers' homes.

Wind whipped on the ferry
I don't think about the monster
beneath the bow—running East-West,
buried beneath the bed.
I ignore evidence of beaches raised and lowered.
I rationalize geological time is not my time.

But when the earth shifts
unable to bear the strain any longer,
and fear runs down my face
while looking for my children—
in that one second and not the thousands before,
I understand fully, the need for release.

Early Winter

In December we hike the forest trail behind our home.
Slog through mud and litter of limbs.
Talk about Christmas in animated voices.

We count again the days our children can stay.
Have forgotten the years we relished a weekend
away from them.

Without warning my husband pushes me to the side.
His head bent back until we both pass under.

"Widowmaker" he says.

After a Summer of Wildfires

I.

The sky is not ablaze.
Flame has gone from high to low.
Hills still smolder.
Beneath cauterized earth
soft melt of flesh will erupt green.

II.

Mt. Constance is a stunner.
A bridal veil peak at seven thousand feet.
In the car,
I am like a groom,
not wanting this white moment to be over
or to be fooled by a name—

but to inhale
                        deep.

Forest Clearing Villanelle

—from a painting by Emily Carr

To destroy a thing is such an easy leave,
clear cut a forest as all its green still weeps,
then walk the forest floor without a bit of grief.

Listen to the *screamers*, splintered stumps bereaving,
build *tombstones* of themselves, as limbs pile in a heap.
To destroy a thing is such an easy leave.

Then dam, strip, poison and oversee the thief,
as crow caw and bear run and cougar take their leap.
Now walk the forest floor, without a bit of grief.

Emily Carr painted canvas with her seeing,
watched storied totems *into silent nothingness* creep.
To purloin a thing is such an easy leave.

Salal and salmonberry are not about deceit,
nor the Saw-whet Owl in conifers dark and deep.
So watch the forest floor without a bit of grief.

May the Elwha's memory be runs of Silvers heaving,
let us know the moss and fern and where the lichen sleep.
To destroy a thing, is such an easy leave.
So behold the forest floor awaken all your grief.

At The Musée d'Orsay

As I stood in front of *Starry Night*
I absolved my companion his
rush through each exhibit—

quit grind of jaw, forgave
crush of shoulders
and sour breath.

I didn't care I stood too long
or that my friend was waiting.
Sometimes it's important to stop—

to imagine a brush filled with Prussian blue
its earthy taste on your tongue
to see a night *more richly colored than day*

to find
like Vincent
a jewel in the darkness.

Finally Becoming Gaia

What happens when you find yourself not yourself?
When stumbling stiff from slumber you spot a spider

ice skating the mirror above your paste and brush
and half-awake imagine glowing rooms of gossamer

waiting for babies yet unborn? So because you
are tired (or so you think) you leave her be

wondering what dream you forgot that allowed this
sharing of space. Then later, when dressing

for the day you find she has moved to the
porcelain sink—and your first thought is *not*

to put her in a shroud of toilet paper down the
baby Moses river, but instead you imagine

her washing dishes in her own kitchen, and because
you are in a hurry (or so you tell yourself) you let her stay

with all eight arm-legs covered in soap. And later still,
when dusk descends and the light is soft and warm,

you find her retiring in the tub, surprised again
there is no eagerness to stomp her out,

no fear she might decide to bed with you, and in
your calm construct a bed of tissue, in case (like you)

she needs a night of peace.

NOTES

"Pomology Lessons": The word "pomology" is a branch of botany that studies and cultivates fruit.

"Where Pain Takes Flight": The first line in this poem was taken from Seamus Heaney's poem "Mother of the Groom."

"The White Album Summer": Italicized words in this poem are taken from The Beatles' record "The White Album."

"Marshmallow Roast with Celtic Goddess Áine": In early Celtic mythology Áine is associated with the King of Munster—Ailill Aulom, who is said to have raped her. This assault ended in Áine biting off his ear, hence the name Aulom "one-eared," which rendered him unfit to be king.

"From the Archive of Regrets": Italicized words in the ninth stanza are taken from the poem "Burial Of The Black Mare" by Dori Calhoun.

"The Algol Paradox": This title was taken from a Wikipedia entry. Specifically, *the Algol paradox is a paradoxical situation when elements of a binary star seem to evolve in discord with the established theories of stellar evolution.*

"Her Husband Flies on the Stratospheric Observatory for Infrared Astronomy": The Stratospheric Observatory for Infrared Astronomy, also known as SOFIA, is an 80/20 partnership of NASA and the German Aerospace Center (DLR) and *is the largest airborne observatory in the world, capable of making observations that are impossible for even the largest and highest ground-based telescopes.*

"Early Winter": The word "Widowmaker" is a forestry term that describes a detached or broken limb or tree top that is a hazard to forest workers, often causing fatalities.

"*Forest Clearing* Villanelle": This poem was inspired by a painting from artist Emily Carr. Words in italics are taken from her writings.

At The Musée d'Orsay": The painter Vincent Van Gogh wrote a letter to his sister Willemien Van Gogh on September 14, 1888, in which he wrote *I definitely want to paint a starry sky now. It often seems to me that the night is even more richly coloured than the day....* This poem contains a quote from his letter.

About the Author

Ironically, the poetry of Carey Taylor embraces impermanence as a touchstone of substance. With a deft touch her poems acknowledge all that drifts to dust as well as the lure of possibility in every new start. The first poem Carey Taylor remembers vividly was called "The Babes in the Wood" which was read to her by her mother when she was around five-years-old. It evoked such a strong emotion in her that she can still remember burying her head in her mother's side trying to hide her unexpected tears. As a child Carey loved to read poems by Edward Lear and Robert Louis Stevenson and as a teenager she spent hours reading the poetry of E.E. Cummings, Gwendolyn Brooks, William Carlos Williams, and Sara Teasdale. She wrote a few poems in high school for a chapbook, but spent most of her adult life in pursuit of other interests. She has worked a variety of jobs including, waitress, cannery worker, secretary, government budget officer, and middle school counselor in addition to being both a wife and mother. She began writing poetry in earnest seven years ago and was fortunate to workshop her poems with John Willson from Bainbridge Island, and Gary Lilley from the Writers' Workshop in Port Townsend. Both these experiences improved her craft and provided her a writing community. She has been published in regional, national and international publications and was nominated for a Pushcart Prize in 2015. She received a Master of Arts degree from Pacific Lutheran University, and a Bachelor's Degree from Linfield College. Carey Taylor was born in Bandon, Oregon and has lived her entire life on the western edges of Oregon and Washington. She writes about poetry and life at careyleetaylor.com.

About Cirque Press

Cirque Press grew out of *Cirque*, a literary journal established in 2009 by Michael Burwell, as a vehicle for the publication of writers and artists of the North Pacific Rim. This region is broadly defined as reaching north from Oregon to the Yukon Territory and south from there through Alaska to Hawaii – and east to the Russian Peninsula. Sandra Kleven joined *Cirque* in 2012 working as a partner with Burwell.

Our contributors are widely published in an array of journals. Their writing is significant. It is personal. It is strong. It draws on these regions in ways that add to the culture of places.

We felt that the body of work of individual writers could be lost if it were to remain scattered across the literary landscape. Therefore, we established a press to collect the work. Cirque Press (2017) seeks to gather the work of our contributors into book-form where it can be experienced coherently as statement, observation, and artistry.

Sandra Kleven – Michael Burwell, publishers and editors

Books from Cirque Press:
Apportioning the Light by Karen Tschannen (2018)
The Lure of Impermanence by Carey Taylor (2018)
Like Painted Kites by Clifton Bates (2018)
Echolocation by Kristin Berger (2018)

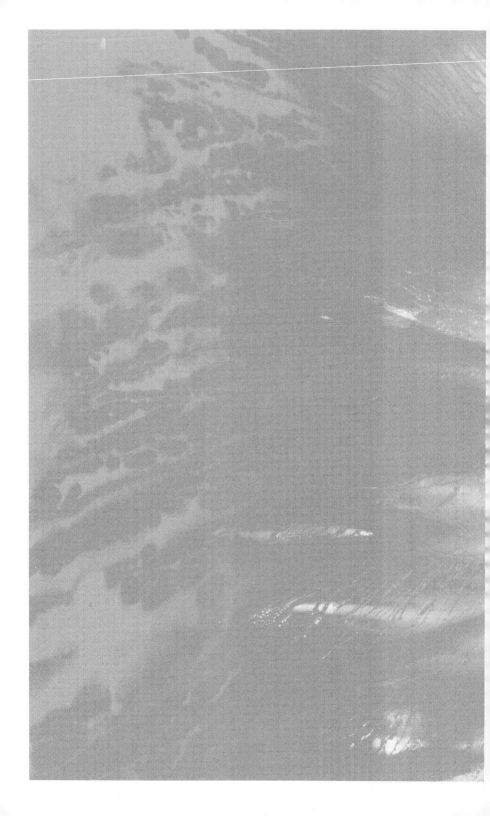

Made in the USA
Columbia, SC
06 August 2018